W · R · I · T · E
THROUGH THE YEAR

by Wanda Lincoln

illustrated by Lisa Levine

FOR MY DAD

Related writing books from Monday Morning Books, Inc.: *Book Factory, Writing Hangups, Greeting Cards, For the Love of Editing, For the Love of Letter Writing, For the Love of Research, For the Love of Stories.*

Publisher: Roberta Suid
Contributing Editor: Murray Suid
Editor: Carol Whiteley
Production: Susan Pinkerton

monday morning®

Monday Morning is a registered trademark of Monday Morning Books, Inc.

ISBN 0-912107-90-1
Printed in the United States of America
9 8 7 6 5 4 3

Contents

good see p. 92, also *end of yr. for open House perhaps*

INTRODUCTION

Like a story, a school year has a beginning, a middle, and an end. Each "season" offers special opportunities for developing and using writing skills. *Write Through the Year* presents projects, games, and bulletin boards that can help you and your students make the most of every moment. Every one of these classroom-tested, whole-language activities:

- provides essential skill practice
- encourages students to reach out to readers
- deals with important learning issues

You will find that regular practice, even if done briefly, can help your students become confident, competent writers.

In addition to step-by-step directions, each activity includes a Learning Bonus that explains how the project links to one or more of the larger issues of quality education, namely:

- self-esteem
- integrated curriculum
- cooperative learning
- critical thinking and problem solving
- independent learning
- creativity

Many of the activities are supported by worksheets. Feel free to duplicate and use them as is, or adapt them for your students.

THE THREE SEASONS

Begin-the-Year activities lay the foundation and spark enthusiasm. Quick and easy projects such as *Alike and Different Introductions, Bulletin Board Factory,* and *Mind Your Mottoes* will help students get to know each other, establish rules for a productive classroom community, become active learners, and begin a variety of ongoing writing practices.

Perk-Up-the-Year activities reinforce and extend the basics while providing an escape from mid-year doldrums. Many of these projects are ongoing and offer greater chances for individualized learning. Examples such as *Do-It-Yourself Report Cards, Greeting Card Service, Hallway Hang-ups,* and *Main Street Museum* encourage students to evaluate themselves, uncover new sources of information, and build self-esteem through public-service writing.

End-the-Year activities celebrate accomplishments and set the stage for future learning. By producing such works as *Autograph Books, Anti-boredom Books,* and *Crystal Ball Letters,* students set new goals and say goodbye to the wonderful year that was.

CALENDAR OF REPORT TOPICS

Write Through the Year focuses on the *school* calendar. But the *ordinary* calendar can also stimulate lots of high-quality writing. For example, Valentine's Day is a prime time for sharpening rhyme and humor skills. Thanksgiving Day invites reflective stories and articles. When the moon is full, that's the moment to schedule a science report on tides.

In addition to those obvious moments, historic events can stimulate research-based writing. At the end of this book, you'll find a "special events" calendar listing research starters for each day of the school year. There, you and your students will discover that every day commemorates something worth learning and thinking and writing about. Examples range from the death of Jacques Cartier (September 1) to the establishment of the African nation of Zaire (June 30).

Going beyond this ready-made events calendar, you may wish to create a classroom calendar that lists dates of local interest. These might include birthdays of everyone in your class, birthdays of the members of the school staff, and events from local history—for example, the date your school was opened. This calendar could stimulate all sorts of writing—for example, each student might send a birthday card to the custodian, or the class might write a proclamation commemorating the town's birthday.

Obviously, this book can't anticipate every writing opportunity. As Eleanor Roosevelt wrote, "If life were predictable, it would cease to be life and be without flavor."

In other words, be ready to make every day a writing day.

PART I
Begin-the-Year Activities

CHAPTER 1
Getting to Know Each Other

ALIKE AND DIFFERENT INTRODUCTIONS

Students pair up and interview each other. One writes a paragraph about their similarities; the other writes a paragraph about their differences.

STEPS TO SUCCESS:

1. Pair students randomly. Include yourself if there's an odd number.

2. Give students a copy of the Alike and Different Planner (next page). Have the two students take turns asking each other questions and writing down the information.

3. Encourage students to think of additional categories, for example, "Favorite fictional hero."

4. Give students time to draft and revise their paragraphs.

5. Have the students use the paragraphs to introduce their partners to the class.

LEARNING BONUS: Students practice the skills of making comparisons and public speaking.

We are both tall and blonde.

Your eyes are blue and mine are green.

ALIKE AND DIFFERENT PLANNER

Name of Partner A:

Name of Partner B:

Take notes as you talk to your partner. Use the notes to write paragraphs about how the two of you are alike and different.

Find 10 ways you are alike and 10 ways you are different. Take turns writing down the facts. Think about such things as:
- number of people in your family
- where you were born
- hobbies, sports, and other activities
- foods you like and foods you hate
- books, music, movies, TV shows
- places you've visited

Ways we are alike:

Ways we are different:

AUTO-MOBILES

Students create mobiles featuring autobiographical shapes and information.

STEPS TO SUCCESS:

1. Tell students that their mobiles will have at least four cut-out shapes and three written cards. Show them an example made by you or a former student.

2. Hand out the Auto-mobile Planner (next page), which lists ideas for the cut-outs and write-ons.

3. After students make their choices, help them create their cut-outs and write-ons.

4. Make the mobile "bodies" by covering wire hangers with wrapping paper. The student's name goes on the body.

5. Attach the cut-outs and write-ons using various lengths of colored yarn. Adjust the placement for balance.

6. Hang the mobiles around the classroom, so students can enjoy them while learning about each other.

LEARNING BONUS: At Open House, these colorful conversation-starters will help parents get to know their children's classmates.

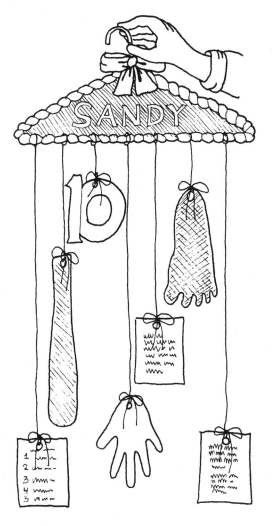

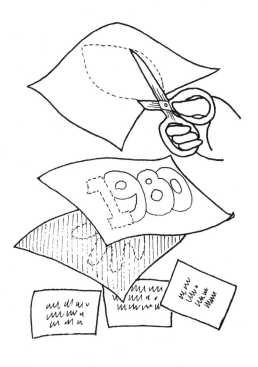

AUTO-MOBILE PLANNER

The word "auto" means self. Your mobile will include shapes and words that tell about you.

SHAPES

Draw and then cut out at least four shapes. Here are some ideas. Try to think of others.

- a flag that could be your symbol

- your footprint

- your hand print

- an object that stands for a hobby or activity, for example, a musical instrument

- the numerals of your birth year

- a shape that stands for your favorite sport

- the shape of your favorite food

WORDS

Choose at least three topics that interest you. On scratch paper write a few sentences about each one. After you revise your work, copy the finished words onto index cards or construction paper. Here are some topics:

- things that interest you

- the best book you ever read

- questions about a subject you'd like to study this year

- your favorite place

- a poem describing your favorite season

SUMMER VACATION WISH BOOK

Students write stories about wished-for summer adventures.

STEPS TO SUCCESS:

1. Lead a class discussion about the real experiences students had during the summer. On the board list activities such as trips, visits from relatives, birthdays, hobbies, and the like.

2. Ask students to imagine adventures they wish they had had—traveling to Mars, digging to China, whatever.

3. Have each student pick an adventure and write about it. To focus the action, suggest that each author draw a picture of a key scene from the story. For further help, have the students use the Adventure Planner (next page).

4. Encourage each student to read the rough draft to a partner. This can be a big help in revising the story.

5. Bind the final copies into a class book for all to read and enjoy.

LEARNING BONUS: This activity—which works equally well following weekends or holidays—enables you to assess important writing skills, such as sequencing and using details.

ADVENTURE PLANNER

Answer the following questions to create a good story.

1. Where does your story take place? Include details.

2. Who are the main characters in your story? (Characters include people and animals.)

3. What happens at the beginning of your story?

4. What does your main character want to do?

5. What are some of the main events in your story?

6. What happens to your main characters at the end of the story?

On the back of this paper, draw a picture of at least one exciting scene from your story.

IMPORTANT THING POEMS

Students write autobiographical poems using the pattern found in Margaret Wise Brown's classic *The Important Book* (Harcourt, Brace, 1949).

STEPS TO SUCCESS:

1. Read *The Important Book* to the students. On the board, outline the pattern:

The important thing about (name) is_____.
It is true that he/she is_____.
He/she_____.
He/she_____.
He/she_____.
He/she_____.
And he/she_____.
But (repeat line 1)_____.

2. Lead the class in creating an "important poem" based on a topic everyone is familiar with, for example, the principal, recess, or autumn. Here is a sample:

The important thing about Mrs. Ho is that she
    says "Hi" when she sees us.
It is true that she is tall.
She listens to classical music on her stereo.
She keeps fresh flowers on her desk.
She reads to us at assemblies.
She knows everyone's name.
And she has been principal of our school for five
    years.
But the important thing about Mrs. Ho is that she
    says "Hi" when she sees us.

3. Help students compose "important poems" about themselves.

4. Have students revise and then illustrate their poems. Bind the poems into a book in which students can read about their classmates.

LEARNING BONUS: Students will have a taste of writing success using this structured pattern, which can be easily adapted for all subject areas.

The important thing about autumn? Leaves changing colors...

I QUIZZES

Students write questions and answers to create quizzes about themselves.

STEPS TO SUCCESS:

1. For a model, create a quiz about yourself. Write both true/false and multiple-choice questions. Then answer them. For example:

I like:
   A. sailing
   B. golfing
   C. eating
   D. all of the above

Answer: D. I do all of these things whenever possible. Eating is the only one that can be done throughout the year, so it's my favorite.

2. Next, have each student list about 20 autobiographical facts, for example:

I have three sisters.
I hate bubble gum.
I have been inside the Statue of Liberty.

3. Ask students to choose the 10 most interesting facts and then write a mixture of true/false and multiple-choice questions about those facts.

4. Have students write a few sentences that explain each yes/no or true/false answer.

5. After final editing, ask students to copy their questions onto a sheet of paper and the answers onto the back. For interest, suggest adding art and borders.

6. After students exchange quizzes with their classmates, display the quizzes on a bulletin board or bind them into a class quiz book.

LEARNING BONUS: This getting-to-know-you activity exercises the thinking skill of composing questions.

16

KNOW-ME WORD SEARCHES

Students create grids filled with words about themselves.

STEPS TO SUCCESS:

1. Have the class brainstorm 15 or 20 questions that everyone can answer, for example:

What is your favorite food?
What is your best school subject?
Who is an author that you like to read?
What is your favorite game?
What animal would you most like to be?
In which month were you born?

2. Show students how to fit their one-word answers into a grid. Words may be placed vertically, horizontally, or diagonally, and they may intersect.

3. After filling in as many answers as possible, have students write random letters in the empty squares.

4. Duplicate the word searches and make them available for students to work on in their spare minutes.

5. When a student tries another student's grid, the results should be given to the author for checking.

LEARNING BONUS: This activity offers a way to make productive use of spare minutes. It also gives students practice in correcting each other's work.

OUR CINQUAINS

Students write autobiographical poems using the cinquain format.

STEPS TO SUCCESS:

1. Write a model autobiographical cinquain on the board, and read it aloud to help students grasp the five-line pattern:

Mr. Blier

Bearded, humorous

Talking, listening, guiding

He loves this school.

Teacher

2. Hand out the Cinquain Planner (next page). Explain the pattern line by line:

    Line 1. Name of poet

    Line 2. Two adjectives describing the poet

    Line 3. Three "ing" verbs (singing, running, etc.) telling favorite activities

    Line 4. A four-word sentence giving an important fact

    Line 5. A noun describing or renaming the poet

3. Help students plan and draft their poems.

4. When students have finished their drafts, pair them for editing. Ask them to begin by reading the poem aloud. Encourage editing partners to ask questions and make suggestions, which the poets can accept or not.

5. Have students illustrate final versions and then work together to create a poetry bulletin board.

LEARNING BONUS: This activity introduces students to the important process of peer editing.

CINQUAIN PLANNER

The following steps will help you get ready to write a cinquain poem.

1. List 10 adjectives that describe you, for example: tall, silly, happy.

Circle two of the adjectives.

2. List 12 "-ing" verbs that describe actions you do well, for example: swimming, reading, joking, etc.

Circle three of the verbs.

3. Write three four-word sentences or phrases that tell something important about you.

Circle one of the sentences.

4. List four nouns that describe you.

Circle one of the nouns.

TIME LINE HANG-UPS

Students create time lines that display autobiographical information year by year.

STEPS TO SUCCESS:

1. Show students a time line of your life. (You might want to use intervals of three or four years to keep the length manageable.)

2. For homework, have students interview their parents to learn about several events from each year of their own lives. For example, a child's third year might include a first plane ride, a broken hand, and a trip to the seashore.

3. Pair the students and have partners help each other choose one significant event for each year.

4. Help the students make their time lines on large sheets of paper or poster board. To add interest, have them paste on relevant artifacts, for example, a bandage could represent a medical problem.

5. Have each student come up with a unique title, for example, "Murray's Memorable Moments."

6. Put up all time lines to create an inviting personal history bulletin board.

7. Try repeating the activity with students creating time lines for famous people.

LEARNING BONUS: This project provides practice in interviewing — a real-world research technique.

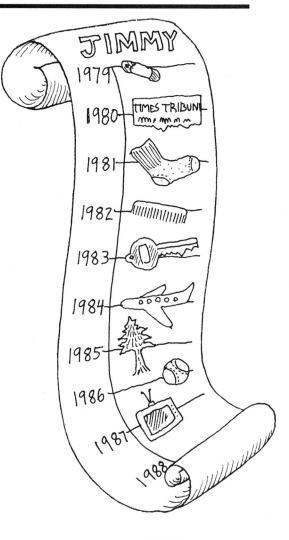

CHAPTER 2

Creating a Community

CLASSROOM CENSUS

Students conduct a census of the classroom's citizens.

STEPS TO SUCCESS:

1. Have the class brainstorm one census-type question for each child in the room. Examples are:

Have you ever seen an ocean?

What is your favorite food?

How many letters are in your last name?

What is your main job (chore) at home?

What is your birth month?

How many syllables are in your first and last names?

If you have a pet, what kind is it?

2. Have each student pose his or her question to every member of the class and record the answers. Encourage students to ask follow-up questions, such as, "What was the name of the ocean you saw?"

3. Discuss the process of collecting data. Were there any problems? If so, how might they have been avoided?

4. Teach the class how to write one-paragraph data reports. Here's an example at the fifth grade level:

I asked, "What is your favorite music?" Twenty-two out of 25 students liked rock music best. Six of these liked heavy metal. The rest liked pop. The other three students liked classical music best. While asking my question, I also found out that 11 people take music lessons.

5. Teach students to make bar graphs of their data.

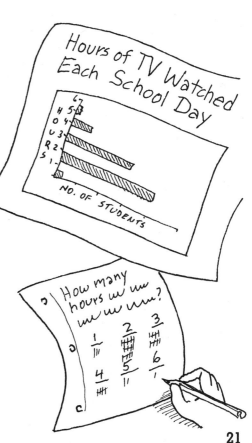

6. Mount the summary paragraphs and graphs back to back on construction paper. Bind the pages into a class book.

LEARNING BONUS: This integrated writing and math activity requires each student to speak with every student in the class.

WELCOMING ACRONYMS

Students create acronyms about a positive learning environment.

STEPS TO SUCCESS:
1. Brainstorm with the class a list of positive classroom behaviors or roles, such as, "think," "care," "question," "share," and "friend."

2. Divide students into small groups. Assign each group a word to turn into an acronym, for example:
   PAL = People Assisting Learning
Hint: The task may be easier if students have access to thesauruses and dictionaries.

3. Have each group make a poster or banner featuring the acronym and an appropriate illustration.

4. Display the acronyms on a classroom bulletin board.

5. Each day or week, randomly choose one of the acronym banners and mount it by the door as a greeting to people who visit your room.

LEARNING BONUS: The acronyms will be ready reminders of positive behaviors.

ENCYCLO-READIA

Students publish book recommendations for their classmates.

STEPS TO SUCCESS:

1. Make many copies of the Book Recommendation Guide (next page).

2. Ask a student (or a small group) to hole punch the copies, place them in a binder, write a title, and create an inviting cover for the book.

3. Encourage students to complete recommendations whenever they finish reading an enjoyable book.

4. Keep the encyclo-readia on an accessible shelf in your room, or place it on the school library's reference shelf for other classes to use.

LEARNING BONUS: This activity helps students learn that their opinions have value. Once they get the hang of it, they might create other recommendation books for movies, games, restaurants, or the like.

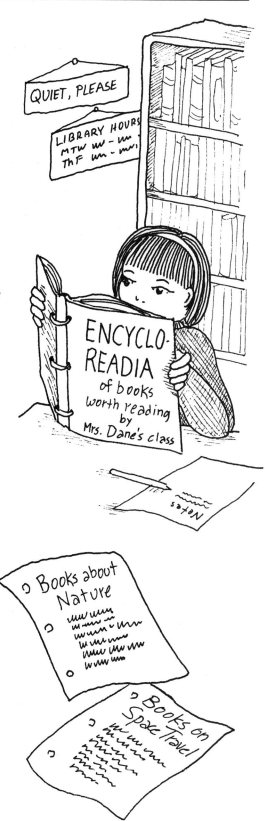

BOOK RECOMMENDATION GUIDE

1. Reader's name:

2. Book title:

3. Author of book:

4. Type of book (fiction, nonfiction, poetry, drama):

5. Description of book's plot or contents:

6. Reasons for recommending this book:

7. Kind of person who would like this book:

8. Additional information (for more space, use back of this sheet):

CLASSROOM MAILBOXES

Students and teachers establish an in-class postal service.

STEPS TO SUCCESS:
1. Help each student choose a type of classroom mailbox to make. Options include:
   - boxes with slits in the covers
   - file folders tacked to a bulletin board
   - plastic sandwich bags taped to the desks

2. Show students how to make their mailboxes.

3. Present suggestions for in-class letters and memos. Possibilities are:
   - asking the teacher or a classmate for help with a lesson
   - thanking someone for a favor
   - commenting on a filmstrip
   - giving the teacher a suggestion, for example, about a class outing
   - sharing enthusiasm for a book or movie

4. Post and discuss guidelines for mail etiquette. Some typical rules are:
   - All mail must be signed.
   - All mail will, if possible, be answered by the following school day.

5. Arrange for a time when students can post their letters, for example, on the way to lunch.

LEARNING BONUS: Students practice writing for a real purpose. Also, they can communicate with the teacher without interrupting a lesson.

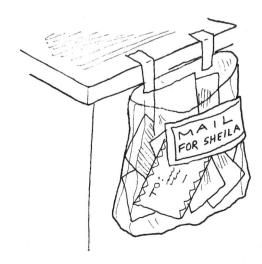

PAGE-A-WEEK YEARBOOK

Throughout the year different students create weekly reports of important classroom events. Each report becomes part of an emerging yearbook.

STEPS TO SUCCESS:

1. Explain the project by presenting a model yearbook page with features such as:
- a paragraph about the major lessons of the week or about an extra-curricular activity
- a captioned picture (photograph or drawing) of an important event, for example, a poetry reading in the library

2. Assign each student one or two weeks to cover during the year. (Have a student create a poster that will remind reporters when their assigned weeks come up.)

3. To prepare students for their reporting tasks, do the first week's page as a group project.

4. Have the class create a title for the yearbook.

5. Form a committee to create a cover and title page.

6. Each Monday, meet with the current reporter to preview the week's planned events. You might suggest ideas for the weekly picture.

7. Each Friday, check the report, ask for revisions—if necessary—and enter the page into the yearbook binder.

8. Encourage students to read the book as the year goes along.

LEARNING BONUS: Reading this ongoing record of highlights will give students a sense of their own history and progress.

CLASSROOM EXPEDITION REPORTS

After locating various classroom resources, students write impressions of the classroom and share questions.

STEPS TO SUCCESS:

1. Ask students to survey the room from their seats. Point out displays and materials.

2. Hand out the Classroom Expedition Record Sheet (next page). Before duplicating the form, fill in the items that are actually available in your room, for example:
- construction paper
- globe
- homework in-box
- reference books
- posted rules
- writing center
- tape recorders

You might do the first entry on the board.

3. Assign students different places to start on the list and then give them a time limit—say, five minutes—for investigating the items.

4. At the end of the time, go over the answers and discuss rules that apply to the use of each item.

5. On separate pieces of paper, have students compose paragraphs giving their impressions of the classroom. These paragraphs can also include questions, for example:

> There are lots of things to use in the room. My favorite is the microscope. I've never used one before. I can't wait to try it. I wonder how often we'll have science?

6. As students share their paragraphs, you can answer their questions.

LEARNING BONUS: This activity lets you see your room from the students' perspective. Send the reports home to tell parents about your program.

CLASSROOM EXPEDITION RECORD SHEET

Look for the classroom resources listed on the left. When you find one, write its location in the right-hand column. On the back of this sheet, write any questions you have.

	Resource	**Location**
1.		
2.		
3.		
4.		
5.		
6.		
7.		
8.		
9.		
10.		

WE, THE LEARNERS

Students compose a learner's "Bill of Rights and Responsibilities."

STEPS TO SUCCESS:
1. Help the class draft a list of the rights and responsibilities of a classroom learner. Here's a fifth grade example:

Rights
- to learn
- to feel safe
- to ask questions
- to make learning choices
- to have a chance for sharing ideas and work
- to make mistakes without getting laughed at

Responsibilities
- to respect the work of other students
- to help classmates
- to listen when being talked to
- to cooperate on group projects
- to share materials and knowledge
- to clean up

2. Post both lists in a prominent place so students can think about them.

3. A day or two later, review and revise the lists. Then have the students make illustrated posters of the final versions.

4. Have students make copies of the rights and responsibilities to share with their parents.

LEARNING BONUS: Students learn that membership in a group involves both rights and responsibilities. The two lists also reinforce classroom discipline guidelines.

EXPERTS BOOK

Students write a resource book that offers all sorts of curricular and extra-curricular support.

STEPS TO SUCCESS:
1. Have the class brainstorm a list of skills they have. Examples are:
   • how to punctuate sentences
   • how to operate the filmstrip projector
   • how to use the word processor
   • how to find books in the library
   • how to study new spelling words

2. Next, brainstorm a list of topics that the students know something about:
   • dinosaurs
   • paper airplanes
   • Texas
   • amusement parks
   • braces

3. Have each student create a page for the book. List the topic or skill at the top followed by lines on which students will sign their names if they qualify as experts. Include a piece of art.

4. Put the pages in a loose-leaf binder to make a classroom book. Have students list their names as helpers on appropriate pages.

5. Keep the book in a convenient location. Throughout the year, encourage students to use the book whenever they need help. Add additional pages as new skills are developed and new topics studied.

LEARNING BONUS: Students have the opportunity to share their knowledge. They also learn that there's more than one teacher in every classroom.

BULLETIN BOARD FACTORY

Students design and create bulletin boards for the classroom and the entire school.

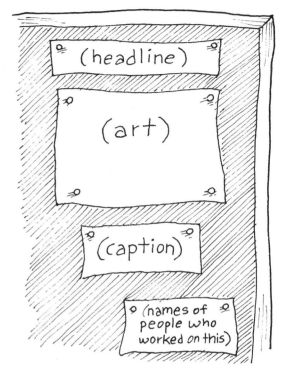

STEPS TO SUCCESS:

1. Take an in-school field trip to study bulletin boards in hallways and other rooms. Have students take notes on the subjects; have them sketch the different layouts.

2. Discuss the major elements found in most boards:
   • content or theme
   • title
   • text: words about the whole board and captions for art that needs explaining
   • lettering (by hand, typed, cut out, computer printed)
   • art (shapes, colors)
   • border

3. Have students practice board-making skills by helping you produce a group-made board for your room. Choose an important subject, for example, a lesson about the Dewey Decimal System. Use the Bulletin Board Planner (next page) to guide this initial exercise.

4. When the board is complete, give students recognition by displaying a card with their names on the board.

5. Have the students write an advertisement for a board-making service. Let them offer their skills to the principal, nurse, or other teachers.

LEARNING BONUS: Students learn to work together while contributing to the classroom environment and the school community.

BULLETIN BOARD PLANNER

1. Describe the subject of the board in one or two sentences.

2. Choose the type of board: display of information, quiz, game, other.

3. List the illustrations—drawings, photos, student work, maps, etc.—that will appear on the board.

4. Make a simple sketch of the board on the back of this sheet. This should include where the title will go, where the art will go, and where the captions will go.

5. Create or gather the art.

6. Write the title for the board. It should have only a few words, but these should grab the reader's attention.

7. Write the text for the board on the back of this sheet: words that go with the art and words that explain the entire board. There should also be a credit box.

8. Neatly copy the title and other text.

9. Put up the board. If the parts don't look just right, move them around.

10. Stand back and watch what happens when people notice the board.

CLASSROOM ASSISTANTS BOOK

Students help with jobs often done by the teacher.

STEPS TO SUCCESS:

1. Have the students list jobs that must be done to keep the classroom running smoothly. Enrich their list by drawing on your own experiences and from the Classroom Roles sheet (next page).

2. Assign each student the task of writing a job description for one of the items on the list. The description might include the following:
    • how to do the job
    • when (how often) the job should be done
    • materials needed to do the job

3. After revising the text, have students copy the final version, with art, onto clean paper.

4. Assemble the pages into a Classroom Assistants Book.

5. Create a responsibility chart that lists each student's job for the week.

6. When students get new ideas about how to do their jobs, they can write suggestions on the backs of the appropriate pages in the book.

LEARNING BONUS: Helping run the classroom teaches students responsibility and encourages them to do things for themselves.

CLASSROOM ROLES

Line leader

Lunch monitor

Greeter (answers the door so that the teacher is not interrupted)

Announcements reader

Sign maker

Special program monitor (reminds students of pull-out programs)

Researcher (finds answers to questions that come up during class)

Botanist (waters plants)

Games keeper (makes sure puzzle pieces are replaced, etc.)

Story reader (reads aloud from book of the week)

News reporter (summarizes major current events news of the day)

Library aide

Audio-visual consultant (operates equipment)

Homework collector

Paper passer (hands back work)

Finder (helps teacher look for lost papers, etc.)

Clean-up aide

Librarian (keeps track of in-class library materials)

Board cleaner

Catcher-upper (tells absent kids what they missed)

Set-up staffer (arranges materials for projects)

Lunch counter

Locker checker

Light controller (makes sure lights are out when room is empty)

Nurse (hands out bandages)

Attendance checker

Calendar checker (makes sure appointments are kept)

Mail person (delivers in-class mail)

Pencil distributor

Substitute assistant (handles a job when a worker is absent)

Responsibility supervisor (checks to make sure the jobs are done)

CHAPTER 3

Learning about Learning

MIND YOUR MOTTOES

Students create phrases, sentences, or rhymes about learning.

STEPS TO SUCCESS:

1. Discuss the kind of values and strategies that help a person become a successful learner.

2. Give students sample mottoes which you have written or have saved from previous years. A motto can take various forms, including that of an imperative sentence:

Learn something new every day.

Or a declarative sentence:

My classmates are my teachers.

Or even a short rhyme:

If you want
To pass that test,
Study hard
Before you rest.

3. Have each student write several mottoes and then choose his or her favorite.

4. Encourage students to write their mottoes on their homemade book jackets or notebook covers.

5. Each week, choose one of the student's mottoes for use as a class motto. Display it on a poster or attach it to the classroom door.

LEARNING BONUS: Making a learning-related motto helps students think about the many aspects of going to school.

CLASS SPELLING GUIDE

Students contribute to a book of words they have mis-spelled. The book contains memory tricks to help everyone master these tricky words.

STEPS TO SUCCESS:

1. Bring in a loose-leaf binder with alphabet separations. Have a committee create a title and cover for the book.

2. When a spelling error has been identified in a paper, the student should write the word correctly in his or her own spelling notebook. Next to the entry, the problem should be stated. For example:

   "Writing" has only one "t" in it, not two.

3. The student should then invent a memory trick for remembering the correct spelling. This can be done by linking the difficult word to one that the student already knows how to spell. For example:

   To write "writing" right, remember that "write" contains only one "t."

4. After revising the sentence, have the student prepare a page for the Class Spelling Guide using a standard format. For example:
   • the problem word spelled correctly at top of page
   • the sentence that explains the problem
   • the memory trick sentence
   • art that helps emphasize the correct spelling

5. The page should then be inserted into the Class Spelling Guide. (For more spelling trick ideas, see *Demonic Mnemonics*, published by David S. Lake.)

LEARNING BONUS: Keeping track of errors—and thinking up memory tricks—is one of the best ways of mastering correct spelling.

MY EVALUATION CALENDAR

Students write observations, opinions, and questions about each school day and each week.

STEPS TO SUCCESS:

1. At the beginning of the week give the students the My Evaluation Planner (next page). The first time, show how to use the form by helping students list responses.

2. At the end of each day, guide the students as they write independently. On some days students may wish to share their statements or questions.

3. On Friday, help students complete the weekly self-evaluation portion of the planner.

4. After you have reviewed the calendars, send them home with other class papers.

LEARNING BONUS: This activity requires that students use writing to evaluate themselves.

MY EVALUATION PLANNER

For the week of_____

Name_____

	Monday	Tuesday	Wednesday	Thursday	Friday
Two things I learned or practiced					
My opinion of the day					
A question I have					

End-of-the-Week Thoughts

1. My favorite activity was _____ because

_____

2. I think I need to work on _____

3. I made progress with _____

4. I read about _____

HOW-I-LEARN SUMMARIES

Students observe and write about the many ways they learn.

STEPS TO SUCCESS:

1. Hand out the How-I-Learn Planner. Discuss the directions. Have the students complete this pre-writing activity.

2. Use the filled-in planners to prepare students for observing their own learning.

3. Have students keep a record of their learning activities for a day or two. A fourth grader might write:

> I listened to a tape and learned a new story.
>
> In math I worked with graphs. It was hard, but Jan helped me get it.
>
> I learned that I knew a lot of spelling words when I took the pre-test.

4. Later, help students compose summaries of what they found out from their observations.

5. Divide the class into small groups, and have the students read their summaries to each other. You might share your style and patterns, too.

LEARNING BONUS: Students recognize that learning takes place in many ways. This builds understanding of self and others.

HOW-I-LEARN PLANNER

Name:

Choose one or more answers for each item.

1. I like to learn something new by:
___ reading more about it
___ hearing someone tell about it
___ seeing pictures of it
___ trying it out myself

2. To remember something I:
___ write it in my own words
___ draw a picture of it
___ explain it to someone
___ try a memory trick
___ have someone test me

3. The learning activities I like best are:
___ small groups
___ whole class
___ working with a partner
___ working by myself
___ working on a learning team
___ listening
___ playing a learning game
___ doing an experiment
___ reading a textbook
___ doing practice papers (ditto sheets)
___ watching a film or video
___ being in a classroom with students talking to each other
___ being in a quiet classroom

4. I like:
___ sometimes taking a break from my work
___ sharing learning materials
___ helping others
___ talking in front of the class
___ asking questions
___ doing homework
___ keeping my desk neat

PART II
Perk-Up-the-Year Activities

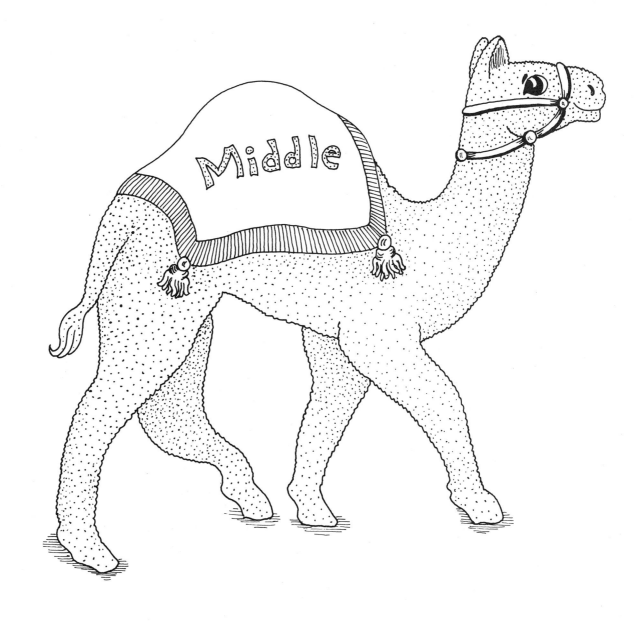

CHAPTER 4

Taking Stock

CONFERENCE INTRODUCTIONS

Students tape-record comments about their school work. The tapes are then used at parent-teacher conferences.

STEPS TO SUCCESS:

1. Hand out the Interview Planner (next page). Explain that students will use the planner to write a script that they will then tape-record.

2. Ask students to compose answers to the questions on the planner. They can also think up their own questions.

3. After students revise and rehearse their responses, pair the students and have them rehearse with their partners. The partner should ask the questions and the author should read the answers.

4. Schedule time for each pair to record their interviews on audiotape or videotape.

5. Use the tapes to begin parent conferences.

LEARNING BONUS: These self-evaluations enable students to participate in the parent-teacher conferences. They also make good icebreakers at conference time.

Hi, Mom and Dad. Welcome to the conference. Before you talk to Mrs. Walker, here is an interview about my work.

INTERVIEW PLANNER

Author's name:

Interviewer's name:

(Write your answers on another piece of paper.)

1. Write a few sentences welcoming your parent or parents to a meeting with your teacher.

2. Write answers to at least five of the following questions. You can also add your own questions to answer. Each answer should be at least three sentences long.

    A. What have you enjoyed learning?

    B. What subject is the most difficult for you? Explain.

    C. What are three things you like about school this year?

    D. What three things would you like to change?

    E. What has made you proud this year?

    F. How has your behavior been in class?

    G. How are your study and work habits? Give an example.

    H. What plans do you have to improve your progress during the rest of the year?

3. Write a few sentences that end your script. One idea would be to read a few lines from something that you wrote in class.

4. Practice reading your answers aloud with your partner. Then record your interview.

DO-IT-YOURSELF REPORT CARDS

Students write evaluations of their work.

STEPS TO SUCCESS:

1. Look at the Do-It-Yourself Report Card form (next page). Adapt it for your students.

2. Discuss the importance of self-evaluation in the learning process. Then distribute the forms to the class.

3. Guide students as they draft their evaluations. For example, in the reading section, give students a list of topics to comment on:
   • participation in the Sustained Silent Reading program
   • favorite type of reading
   • new vocabulary
   • ability to predict events in a story

4. Direct students to edit their reports for content and mechanics. Then have them copy the final versions onto the Report Card forms.

5. Ask the students if they will allow you to read their evaluations. Do so when permitted.

6. Send the student evaluations home with your own report card. Encourage parents to discuss both reports with their children.

LEARNING BONUS: Students learn that self-evaluation is an important learning tool, and parents get a more complete picture of their child's education.

45

DO-IT-YOURSELF REPORT CARD

Name:

Reading	Math
Spelling	Projects and goals
Science	Handwriting
Writing	Self-control
Special classes	My favorite learning activity
My opinion of the year so far	Things I'd like to change

PORTFOLIO REPORTS

Students assemble a sampler of their work.

STEPS TO SUCCESS:

1. Choose an area for the portfolios, for example: art, problem solving, writing, etc.

2. List three or four criteria of excellence for the type of work. For example, with story writing, the list might include:
   - original title
   - interesting beginning
   - well-described characters
   - exciting action
   - strong mechanics (spelling, punctuation)

3. Have students choose two or three examples of their work that they are proud of.

4. Have students write one paragraph about the type of work in the portfolio. In a short story portfolio, for example, the paragraph might list the elements of a short story.

5. Students should then write a second paragraph that discusses the specific examples in the portfolio. This second paragraph might explain what is strong about the work.

6. Have the students take their portfolios home to share with their parents.

LEARNING BONUS: A portfolio report offers parents tangible evidence of their child's efforts and progress.

I'm going to show you some of my best work.

FRONT PAGE NEWS

Students turn their learning accomplishments and goals into real news.

STEPS TO SUCCESS:

1. Bring in sample front pages from your local newspaper. Discuss the elements:
- masthead (title of paper and date)
- main story (usually printed in the upper right hand portion of the page)
- other stories
- headlines and subheads
- bylines
- photos or drawings

2. Explain that each student will create a personal newspaper front page that reviews the school year to this point and that also looks ahead.

3. Have each student list eight or ten article ideas that cover accomplishments and future plans, for example:
- long division learned
- field trip to art museum
- science fair to be held in March

4. Help students draft five or six news stories. As in most good newspaper stories, the first paragraph should offer a summary by answering all or most of the five "w" questions: who, what, where, when, and why.

5. Have students revise their articles, sketch the front page layouts, and then make final copies. For an authentic newspaper look, use large sheets of paper. If possible, use a personal computer that has a desktop publishing program.

6. Send the papers home as newsy responses to the question, "What have you learned in school lately?"

LEARNING BONUS: Students assess their work for their parents while learning about an important communication format.

SYLVIA'S SENTINEL

DECEMBER

Long Division Mastered

Book fair to feature work by Sylvia Miller and others

SCIENCE PROJECT PLANNED FOR SPRING

CLASSROOM TOUR GUIDE

Students write directions to help parents get the most out of their classroom visits.

STEPS TO SUCCESS:

1. Discuss the reasons for inviting parents to visit the classroom:
- to help parents understand the program
- to give parents a feel for the environment
- to improve parent-teacher communication

2. Explain what a self-guided tour sheet is. You might use an example from a zoo or museum, or write one yourself. Go over the basic elements:
- description of key points to visit (in order)
- map (optional)

3. Have each student identify half a dozen important places in the room. The list should include his or her own desk or a project that is on display.

4. Have students draft short paragraphs about each landmark.

5. After editing, the paragraphs should be copied onto a guide sheet, along with appropriate illustrations.

6. Give parents their children's guide sheets whenever they visit the room.

LEARNING BONUS: Students learn to look at their environment with a critical eye as they interpret the room for their parents.

CHAPTER 5
Adding Zest

DAILY QUICK LISTS

Students practice brainstorming by writing lists of words that relate to a given topic.

STEPS TO SUCCESS:

1. List categories that are appropriate for your class. Examples are:
- synonyms for "said"
- things that are both hard and soft
- color words
- things kept in a cage

For more ideas, see the next page.

2. Explain the rules of "quick listing" to your class:
- The goal is to list as many words or phrases as you can think of that fit the topic.
- You may work alone or with a partner.
- It is not a contest, so you may share ideas.
- Because the list is a rough draft, spelling and handwriting are not important. Ideas are what count.

3. Demonstrate the activity:

Things People Collect

plates	post cards
records	dolls
insects	baseball cards
ticket stubs	bumper stickers
toy soldiers	stuffed animals
tin foil	bad jokes

4. Do the activity on a regular basis—daily, if possible. Usually, give a specific time period, say, three minutes. Occasionally, let students work without a time limit.

LEARNING BONUS: Making quick lists develops fluent thinking—a key to creativity.

QUICK LIST TOPICS

kinds of boats
types of minerals
things that can be filled
careers
names for young animals
words for sounds (bang, hiss)
cities
clothing
types of litter
parts of an automobile
vegetables
things worth over $1000
things worth less than a dime
names of countries
types of houses
pets
things we can get for free
types of coins
things that are red
kinds of sandwiches
things with a motor
holidays
types of toys
ways to say "I like you"
things made with chocolate
things with a door
places to eat

outdoor activities
names of television shows
places to visit in a city
ways to tell time
things that can be locked
things that can be driven
types of jewels
sports
names of authors
palindromes (mom, noon,
    dad, did, pop)
games played in a house
languages
things found in a kitchen
things worn on the head
round things
smooth things
sweet things
things found in the ocean
things found in the forest
things that are good for you
cartoon characters
heroes
things to write with
African animals
things smaller than a shoe box
things that come in pairs

GREETING CARD SERVICE

Students create and send birthday, get well, anniversary, and other greeting cards.

STEPS TO SUCCESS:

1. Have each student create an individual special-events calendar for listing the birthdays, anniversaries, and other important days in the lives of friends and relatives. Regularly have students check their calendars for events that involve card sending.

2. Establish a classwide special events calendar that lists the birthdays of students in the class, plus the birthdays of the school staff—secretary, principal, custodian, resource teachers, and others.

3. Collect and study the various kinds of greeting cards. Types include: accordion, see-through, object, rhyming, jigsaw puzzle, and checklist.

4. Organize the class into a greeting-card production company to serve the school. Possible departments are:
- advertising: to publicize the service
- marketing: to get the orders
- supply: to collect and organize the materials
- writing
- illustrating
- distribution: to deliver the orders

Students should switch roles from time to time.

LEARNING BONUS: Creating greeting cards lets students see that their words can really make a difference in people's lives.

LEARNING BOX EXCHANGE

Students collect a box of artifacts that typify their city or region and then exchange the box for one assembled by students in another part of the country.

STEPS TO SUCCESS:

1. Locate an out-of-city teacher who would like to participate in an artifacts exchange.

2. Brainstorm with the class a list of your city's or region's features. Draw ideas from such categories as:
- geography
- special events
- history
- nationalities
- food
- occupations
- traditions
- architecture
- famous people

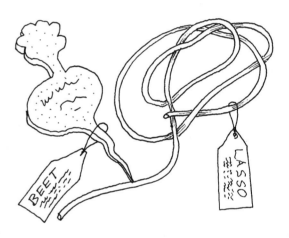

3. Have students create or collect things that represent each category. Encourage students to write at least a paragraph or two about each item.

4. Pack the artifacts and, on a day agreed upon by the cooperating teacher, send the box to the other class.

5. When the exchange box arrives, open it, examine the artifacts, and read the explanations. Have students list facts they learn and questions they have about the box's contents.

6. Have students write a group letter—or individual letters—to the exchange class. Include a summary of what was learned and any questions that need answering.

LEARNING BONUS: This project involves real-world writing and meaningful research. It could even lead to pen-pal friendships.

JUST WRITE DAY

On this day, spoken words are out. Students write notes to communicate throughout the day.

STEPS TO SUCCESS:

1. Assemble the materials that you'll need: a small pad for each student and a signal for attention.

2. Prepare a large sign for the classroom door:
> Today is a special day. We will learn as usual, but we won't use our voices. Enter the room quietly and take a pad. If you have something to "say" to me or a classmate, write it on the pad and sign your name.

3. List the day's activities on the board. Supervise the students as they complete their work and write to each other. Use a pad yourself to send messages to individual students.

4. If necessary, remind students to sign their notes. This will help them be responsible for their words and ideas.

5. The next day—if students can wait that long—have students talk and write about the experience. You might suggest such topics as:
- why the teacher tried the activity
- the differences between writing and talking
- the importance of clear communication

Have students share their reports with parents.

LEARNING BONUS: Students will experience—and maybe acquire a taste for—quiet. They'll also have a chance to practice writing clearly and expressively.

PARENT INVITATIONS

Students write invitations to parents asking them to visit the school for an hour or longer.

STEPS TO SUCCESS:

1. Choose a week and designate it "Parents Come to School Week."

2. Divide the class into five groups, each of which will plan a special program for one day. Possibilities include: book sharing, a puppet show, a science demonstration, or a math lesson.

3. Have each group present its program idea to the rest of the class. The other students should take notes on the various presentations; they'll use the information in their invitations.

4. Guide students as they write their invitations. Each invitation should describe what will happen on each day. It should ask parents to choose one day to visit and then R.S.V.P.

5. Have students write name tags for parents who say they'll come.

6. During the week of visits, the group of the day should act as hosts, guiding guests around the room, explaining the activities, and presenting their special event.

7. Each day, students should write take-home reports about the special event. These reports will be especially valued by parents who were unable to attend.

LEARNING BONUS: Mid-year visits can renew the parents' enthusiasm for your program, and can get students and parents talking about learning.

STARTLING STORY STARTERS

Students create story starters with involving situations, characters, and problems for class use.

STEPS TO SUCCESS:
1. Read aloud several story starters. Discuss which elements are usually provided, for example:
   - main character (protagonist)
   - problem the main character must deal with (may be another person—antagonist)
   - setting
   - initial action

2. Have students choose some or all of these elements and draft their own story starters. Here's an example:

> On a trip to Hawaii, Dan, 10 years old, went on a sailboat ride with his mom. Soon the skies darkened. A typhoon was coming.

3. Have students write their final versions on large index cards. They can add illustrations if they like. On the back, they should list the elements which they have included (protagonist, problem, etc.) and ask one or two questions that the author must answer to complete the story. Each card should carry its creator's name.

4. When the story starters are ready, have students swap them, finish the stories, and share them. The starter starters should then be placed in a box in the writing center.

LEARNING BONUS: Students provide materials for the class while enjoying the stories based on their ideas.

The phone rang. John wondered

HALLWAY HANG-UPS

Students display thought-provoking banners which promote interest in reports published in the library.

STEPS TO SUCCESS:

1. Get the principal's permission to hang banners from hallway ceilings.

2. Consult with the janitor about the means for hanging the banners. (In most cases, masking tape will not harm painted surfaces.)

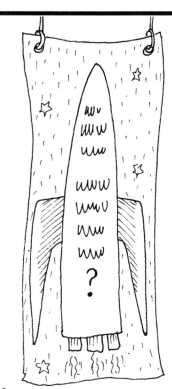

3. Introduce the activity to your class by showing them a sample hang-up, which will include a question and possibly an illustration. For example, the question "Who was the first woman to fly in space?" might appear in the outline of a rocket.

4. Brainstorm categories for conducting research. Possibilities include inventions, people, landmarks, books, and science.

5. Have each student pick a category and then choose an item within it. The student should then write a question about the topic and a short report—one page or less.

6. Using construction paper have students cut out banners in shapes that are appropriate to their topics.

7. Have the class write a project news release for publication in the school's morning bulletin. Then, put up several hang-ups each week, after placing the related reports on display in the library.

LEARNING BONUS: Students contribute to the school's learning environment while giving an extra reason for visiting the library.

CHAPTER 6

Producing Special Events

LITERARY ANTHOLOGY

Students gather their favorite pieces of writing and compile a class book.

STEPS TO SUCCESS:

1. Ask students to choose two or three pieces of writing they have produced during the year. Give them the following criteria:
- You are proud of it.
- It is a good example of your writing skills.
- It will be of interest to readers.

2. Sort the pieces into categories (short stories, poetry, reports, etc.). If any categories have been neglected, request additional pieces.

3. Help the class make the following decisions:
- organization of the material
- number of pages in the issue
- type of print: typing, hand lettering
- method of reproduction
- method of distribution
- anthology title
- dedication
- graphic theme and who will do the illustrations
- cover design

4. Ask for volunteers for the following jobs, which can
be done individually or by committees:
- creating a cover illustration
- producing the title page
- writing a table of contents
- editing each section—poetry, stories, reviews, etc.
- typing the pages (this might be a job for parent
  volunteers or for a typing class)
- drawing borders and illustrations
- numbering the pages
- duplicating and collating the pages
- binding the book
- distributing the book (including donating copies
  to the school and the town libraries)

5. Celebrate the publication with a class party.
Be sure to include school administrators and parents.

LEARNING BONUS: This anthology helps students
feel proud of their writing. It also can be an effective
public relations tool for your writing program.

MAIN STREET MUSEUM

Students, working in small groups, provide information to the community through store window displays.

STEPS TO SUCCESS:

1. Find five or six store owners who are willing to let your students use their windows.

2. Help the class choose a curriculum-related subject or theme that might interest passers-by, for example: animals, books, the future, citizenship, ecology, elections, or weather.

3. Divide the class into groups. Give each group a subject. Have students begin keeping journals in which they will record their plans and progress.

4. Have each group research their topic and then plan a display. The aim will be to educate the general public concerning the subject.

5. Match each group with a store and have the students write a business letter requesting space in the window. The letters should describe the display and should tell how long the window will be used, say, for a week.

6. Help students place their displays in the windows. Consider photographing each one.

7. Have the entire class work on promoting the museum program. Some proven promotion strategies are:
- sending news releases to the local media
- writing letters to the editor of the newspaper
- creating and putting up posters around town
- sending letters to parents
- phoning the chamber of commerce

8. After the displays are taken down, have students write thank-you letters to the stores.

9. Review the project by having students share what they wrote in their journals. Discuss ways that the project might be done better next time.

LEARNING BONUS: Students work cooperatively while learning that their knowledge has value beyond the walls of the school.

CAMPAIGN FOR A GOOD CAUSE

Students use a variety of strategies to promote a worthy cause.

STEPS TO SUCCESS:

1. To help students understand campaigning, discuss political and advertising campaigns. Present artifacts such as posters, buttons, and bumper stickers.

2. Talk about real issues in your school or town that might inspire a campaign. Examples are:
- increasing the percentage of voters in a school election
- convincing the city to put up a stop sign at a dangerous intersection
- trying to get kids to watch less TV
- collecting food for the needy
- urging people to stop littering
- raising money for the school library
- increasing the turnout at Open House

3. Choose an issue and define a specific goal for the campaign, for example:

> We will try to increase the attendance at the next school Open House from 45% to 85%.

4. Schedule the campaign. It might last a week, a month, or until a specific date, for example, the night of the Open House.

5. Brainstorm ways the goal might be achieved:
- circulating a petition
- writing a letter to the mayor
- sending letters to the town newspaper
- putting up posters
- attaching bumper stickers to cars
- handing out leaflets
- getting free public service announcements read on the radio
- giving a "free speech" presentation on the TV
- designing, producing, handing out, and wearing buttons

6. Divide the class into committees. Help each committee break its task into manageable steps, each of which should have a deadline. For example, the bumper sticker committee might:

- generate ideas for a possible sticker
- submit their most convincing idea to the class for evaluation
- produce copies of the bumper sticker
- find people willing to put the stickers on their cars

7. Carry out the campaign.

8. Evaluate the campaign. Which strategies worked? Which ones could have been improved?

LEARNING BONUS: Students develop citizenship skills by trying to make a difference in their world. They also learn first hand how opinions and attitudes can be influenced.

CREATIVE TELEVISION

Students create an educational TV series, producing
cassettes that are sent home for parental viewing.

STEPS TO SUCCESS:
1. Obtain access to a portable videotape camera.
Sources include:
- the school's audio-visual department
- a parent
- a local video shop

2. Brainstorm a list of video program ideas that relate to learning. Possibilities include:
- interviews with students and faculty
- readings of poems, stories, reports, reviews, and essays
- Mr. Wizard-style demonstrations (skills, science experiments)
- songs
- puppet shows
- skits
- in-depth reports about on-going events, such as lunch and student council meetings
- documentaries of unusual happenings, such as field trips and guest visits
- features on gym, music, and other special subjects

3. Teach students the fundamentals of operating the equipment. To practice, divide the class into pairs and have one partner run the camera while the other recites a poem or joke.

4. Break the class into small production groups, each of which will be responsible for a short segment— say, between one and three minutes. Each group will have to do the following:

- Write a script for the segment. A good script—that covers both pictures and sounds—is the key to making a program worth watching.
- Gather the necessary props and backdrops. For example, an interview might require a backdrop giving the title of the show.
- Rehearse the program. Revise the script if necessary.
- Schedule the taping.
- Tape the show.

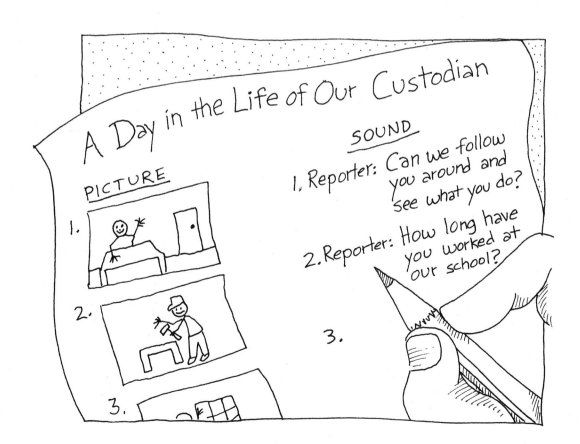

5. Allow students to check the tape out for viewing with their parents. If the parents don't have a videotape machine, have students send them letters inviting them to view the program at school.

6. Later, see if the school library would be interested in circulating the programs as part of its collection.

LEARNING BONUS: Students are able to reach a wider audience for their work while having an active—rather than passive—TV experience.

QUIZ SHOW

Students produce an educational game show for the classroom or the entire school. This format can be used for review of different subjects or current events.

STEPS TO SUCCESS:

1. Introduce the project to your students. If they are interested, help the class create a game show format. It might combine features from several programs.

Note: Many teachers prefer the team approach in which students help each other answer questions. This puts less pressure on individual students. Also, rotating questions between teams rather than using a buzzer guarantees that both sides get a chance to answer without being hurried.

Another way to ease tension is to form teams that consist of both students and adults (teacher, aide, principal, parent).

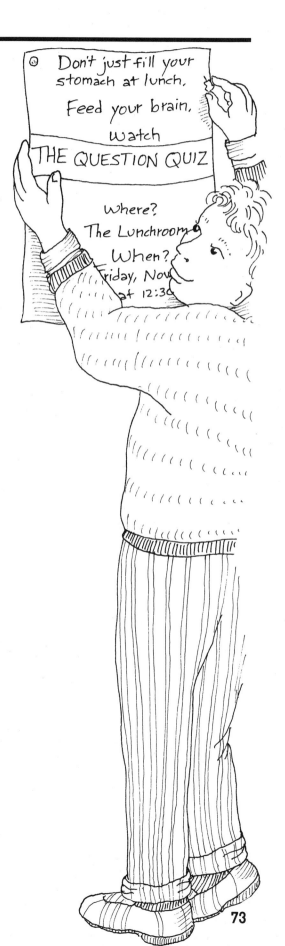

2. Decide on a time and place for the show. For example, if the audience will include students outside your class, you might schedule the program in the cafeteria during the last 15 minutes of lunch. (Hint: When inviting outsiders, stress the idea that viewers should try to figure out answers for themselves, rather than just root for one team or another.)

3. Brainstorm a list of jobs which must be done. Students can rotate through such roles as:
- question writers
- host
- judges who evaluate answers and keep score
- promotion experts who create posters telling when and where the show will be held
- videotape crew (if you decide to "televise" the program)

4. Help the students prepare for the first show. The question writers will probably need the most help. It takes time to come up with questions that aren't too hard and aren't too easy. The questions might review curriculum topics, for example, information covered in the most recently studied science unit.

You could mix in items of common knowledge, for example, "What number should you dial in an emergency?"

Brain stretchers could work, too. For example: "Can you think of a word whose letters are in alphabetical order?" (Answer: *fit*.)

See sample questions at the end of this unit.

5. Hold a dress rehearsal before putting on the first show. Discuss ways for improving the program.

LEARNING BONUS: Presenting a quiz show gives students a chance to combine review, research, and creative thinking for a real purpose.

SAMPLE QUIZ SHOW QUESTIONS

Note: Many of these questions can generate numerous other related questions—for example, spelling words that are often confused, synonyms, number sequences, and fundamental geography facts.

1. Can you name a word whose letters are in alphabetical order?

2. What are five of Canada's provinces?

3. If it's four in the afternoon in New York City, what time is it in Los Angeles?

4. How many players are on the ice during a professional hockey game?

5. What number should you dial if there is an emergency in your home?

6. What is the next number in this progression: 1, 3, 5, 7 . . . ?

7. Can you think of a word that has four syllables?

8. How many teachers work in this school?

9. What is the general Dewey Decimal classification for science?

10. What is the difference between latitude and longitude?

11. At what temperature does water boil on the centigrade scale?

12. In the sentence "It's not my fault," how do you spell "It's."

13. What is the difference between a planet and a moon?

14. What are three synonyms for "say"?

15. If May 16 is on a Sunday, what day of the week is June 1?

16. What do the following words have in common: saxophone, diesel, guillotine? (They're all taken from people's names.)

DIAL-A-READING

Students write and present messages played nightly on an answering machine that is hooked to the school's telephone.

STEPS TO SUCCESS:
1. Propose the project to your class. If the students like it, have them send a letter to the principal asking if the school's phone can be used at night.

2. If the principal agrees, locate a telephone answering machine. While these devices are now relatively cheap—some models cost under $50.00—you might be able to obtain one free. With the help of students, try the following:

- See if the school has one you can borrow.
- Place an ad in the home-school newsletter asking if someone has an old model he or she will give or loan to your class.
- Write a letter to a phone machine store asking for a loaner. Promise to acknowledge the company's generosity in the school's newsletter.

3. Have students list formats suitable to a machine's 30-second or 60-second message length. Possibilities include:

- limericks and other short poems
- school news highlights—for example, a description of a class field trip or an award won by one of the staff
- curriculum reports—for example, a one-minute summary of a science experiment
- reviews of books and movies of interest to families
- home-learning tips
- riddles
- short, short stories

4. Have students, working individually or in small groups, draft, revise, and rehearse presentations.

5. Make a schedule for a month's worth of these telephone presentations. Each program might "play" for two nights.

6. Plan and carry out a public relations campaign. The idea is to alert students, teachers, and parents about the program. Student-created publicity might include:
- posters put up around school
- flyers sent home to parents
- ads placed in the home-school newsletter
- letters to the editor of the town paper

7. Record each program on the day of its "broadcast." Test it before the end of the school day to make sure the words are clear and the pacing right.

8. After a week or so, send an evaluation form home to find out how many people are calling the machine and how they feel about the project.

9. If the results are encouraging, you might invite other classes to participate. You could also send a letter about the program to the local newspaper, suggesting that the paper do an article about the messages.

LEARNING BONUS: Students publish their writing for a large audience and get a chance to use their language skills in a real-world setting.

PART III
End-the-Year Activities

CHAPTER 7

Looking Back

MEMORIES SONG

Using familiar melodies, students write song lyrics about the year.

STEPS TO SUCCESS:

1. Help students list highlights from the year. Make a second list of routines, for example, doing homework or learning the word for the day.

2. Have students nominate tunes that everyone knows and can sing, for example: "I've Been Working on the Railroad," "You Are My Sunshine," "I'm Looking Over a Four Leaf Clover." Then have the class select one.

3. Analyze the rhyming pattern of the chosen song. Next, lead students in composing new lyrics to fit the melody. You might break the class into small groups, each of which writes a verse. Here's an excerpt to the tune "I'd Like to Teach the World to Sing":

> We'd like to tell the whole wide world,
> About our super year!
> We learned a lot and played some, too.
> The facts you will now hear!

4. Ask for volunteers who will sing the drafted lyrics to facilitate editing. Then try the final lyrics as a group and, if necessary, do more editing.

5. Practice the song and perform it for other classes. You might tape it for students to bring home.

LEARNING BONUS: Students review their accomplishments while learning to set words to music.

CLASS HALL OF FAME

Students interview partners and create posters of remembrance and recognition for a goodbye bulletin board.

STEPS TO SUCCESS:

1. Randomly pair students.

2. Have the pairs interview each other, guided by the Hall of Fame Planner (next page).

3. Using that information, each partner completes the following invitation to the Class Hall of Fame.

> Ladies and Gentlemen, I would like to invite_____
> to become a member of our Class Hall of Fame.
> _____deserves this honor because

4. Encourage partners to help each other edit their drafts. Then give guidelines for copying the final versions onto small poster boards. Encourage creative lettering and art.

5. After reading aloud their posters, students should use them to produce a Hall of Fame bulletin board.

LEARNING BONUS: Students practice giving credit where it's due, while you assess growth in interviewing, peer editing, and public speaking.

HALL OF FAME PLANNER

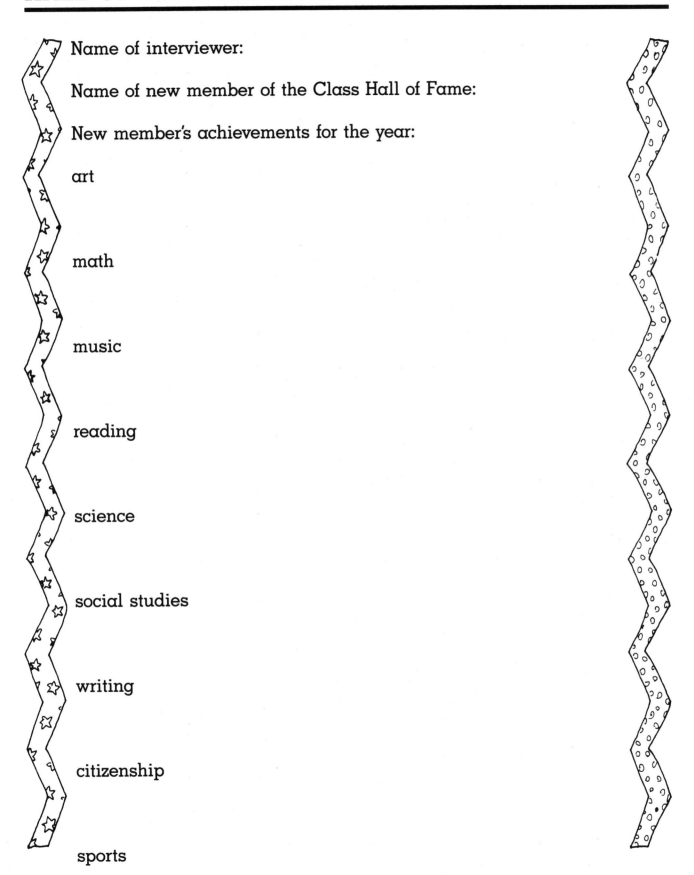

Name of interviewer:

Name of new member of the Class Hall of Fame:

New member's achievements for the year:

art

math

music

reading

science

social studies

writing

citizenship

sports

HOW TO BE A SUCCESS

Students make an advice book that anticipates the questions of next year's students.

STEPS TO SUCCESS:

1. Help the class brainstorm questions that incoming students might ask in September. Topics should include academics and classroom routine. For example:

- Can students sometimes help each other?
- What kinds of jobs are there to do?
- Do we give plays?
- What happens if you don't finish your work?

Urge students to continue listing questions until there is at least one for each student.

2. Assign each student a question. Then hand out copies of the Advice for You Planner (next page). Each student should write his or her question at the top of the page.

3. Tell students to write a one-sentence answer to the question on the first blank, and then pass the sheet to another student who will add a second response. Continue until each question has evoked ten comments. For example:

What should I do when arriving in class?
1. You should say "Hi" to your friends.
2. You should sharpen your pencils.
3. You should try the Daily Challenge.

4. Form a "binding committee" that will:
- put the pages in order, number them, and insert them into a binder
- think up a title
- create a cover and title page
- produce a table of contents

5. In September, invite your new students to read the book and benefit from its advice.

LEARNING BONUS: Students get a chance to use their experiences in a practical way.

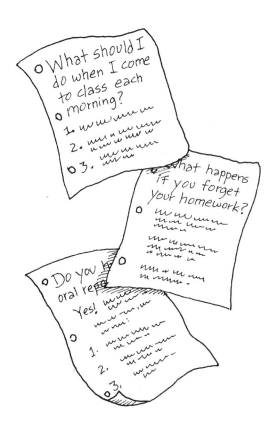

ADVICE FOR YOU PLANNER

Question: _____

_____

	Advice	Advice Giver's Name
1.	_____	_____
2.	_____	_____
3.	_____	_____
4.	_____	_____
5.	_____	_____
6.	_____	_____
7.	_____	_____
8.	_____	_____
9.	_____	_____
10.	_____	_____

HOMEWARD HISTORY

Students write personal history booklets about the school year.

STEPS TO SUCCESS:

1. Brainstorm with the class a list of possible topics for the history booklet. For example:
- how I felt the first day of school
- the best moment of the year
- the worst day
- the funniest time
- the best field trip
- the most interesting guest
- a rule that I would have changed
- the most important thing I learned
- the person who helped me the most
- my favorite subject
- my best writing
- my teachers
- my favorite recess activity
- the time I will never forget
- the time I would like to forget

see p. 92 also

2. Give guidelines for helping students choose topics for their booklets. You might set a minimum number of topics to cover, or list several "must include" items.

3. Show students how to write up each item so it fits on a page. Present a sample so students will know how to develop the topics.

4. Provide time for the students to draft and revise their manuscripts.

5. When it's time to create the final pages, give the students the Personal History Planner (next page). Have ready a variety of art supplies including glue, poster board (for the covers), and binding materials (yarn, rings, ribbon, staples, etc.).

LEARNING BONUS: This booklet sparks conversations between students and parents. It also help students remember their experiences in your class.

PERSONAL HISTORY PLANNER

Use the following checklist as you work on your Personal History booklet.

☐ Cover
This is usually made of cardboard or heavy paper. On the cover will be the title and, if you like, a picture.

☐ Title page
This is the first page. It repeats the title.

☐ Dedication page
This tells who the book is for. Some writers dedicate their books to their parents or friends.

☐ Table of contents
This helps readers find what they are looking for.

☐ Pages within the book
Each page should have a title, border or artwork, and a page number.

☐ Binding
This is what holds the book together. It can be something like yarn, staples, rings, or thread.

WHAT-WE-KNOW-NOW COUPLETS

Students write couplets answering the question, "What did you learn this year?"

STEPS TO SUCCESS:

1. Go over activities and subjects covered during the year. Discuss specific achievements, for example, learning to use a microscope.

2. Present several models prepared by you or other students. Examples are:

In September I could only add and subtract.
Now, in June, I can multiply and divide.

Point out that the first line gives the "before" situation. The second line gives the "after."

3. When students have drafted and sequenced their couplets, have each draft a tag line that sums up the overall sense of achievement, for example:

It wasn't easy, but it was worth it.

4. Have students decorate the page with before and after illustrations for one of the couplets.

5. Use the couplets as an end-of-the-year bulletin board. Students can also present their mini-poems orally to each other or to parents.

LEARNING BONUS: This activity helps students celebrate their achievements.

CHAPTER 8

Looking Ahead

TO-MY-NEXT-TEACHER LETTERS

Students introduce themselves to their next year's teacher by writing a supplement to official records.

STEPS TO SUCCESS:

1. Review the year gone by, reminiscing about topics, projects, programs, and special events.

2. Hand out and discuss the Letter of Introduction Planner (next page). Have students complete the form and note additional information—opinions, goals, and wishes—on the back.

3. Review the friendly letter format, perhaps by writing a letter of your own on chart paper or the overhead.

4. Have students use the planning forms to compose their letters. Have materials available for creating original stationery to be used for the revised draft.

5. Arrange for the letters to be delivered to next year's teacher. (Students moving to another school can take the letters home for delivery in the fall.)

6. Suggest that next year's teachers send "Welcome aboard" responses to your students before school begins.

LEARNING BONUS: This activity gives students an opportunity for self-evaluation, and teaches them how to present themselves through writing.

LETTER OF INTRODUCTION PLANNER

Name:

1. I did my best work this year in

2. I need to learn how to

3. I need more help in

4. The activity I liked best this year was

5. I did not enjoy

6. The book I liked best was

7. This year I wish we had done more

8. My favorite field trip was

9. Next year I am looking forward to

SOMEDAY LISTS

Each student writes a book of life goals.

STEPS TO SUCCESS:

1. Discuss the value of having long-term goals. You might tell about John Goddard who, in his teens, listed 127 dreams he hoped to realize in his life. By age 47 (reported *Life* magazine, 3/24/72), he had reached 103 of the goals, including parachuting from a plane, building a telescope, and learning to play the piano.

2. Help students list goal categories such as:
- places to visit
- people to meet
- sports to master
- books to read
- jobs to work at
- experiences to have
- events to attend
- challenges to meet
- things to see
- subjects to learn

3. Ask each student to list specific goals for 10 or more categories, for example: "I'd like to visit Istanbul" or "I'd like to learn how to play the tuba."

4. Help students write at least a paragraph explaining why each goal is important.

5. After they revise their drafts, have students copy each goal onto its own page, then add art.

6. Have students bind the pages into books, organizing them in some way, for example, from the least to the most important.

7. Encourage students to share their list books with parents and to file the goals for future evaluation.

LEARNING BONUS: This project introduces students to the skills of goal setting and planning.

SUMMER JOURNALS

Students create books to use as journals during vacation.

STEPS TO SUCCESS:

1. Choose the journal format:
- spiral bound
- ring binder
- hand bound

2. Have students bring in or make their blank journals.

3. Explain how journals can be used for recording observations, experiences, feelings, opinions, and questions. A journal is in draft form and can be kept private.

4. Help students create titles and title pages for their journals.

5. Suggest the following organization for the journals:
- Include a page divider for each week of the summer. Use a quotation book to find an encouraging quote to start each week. Use colored pens, crayons, and stick-ons to make borders.
- Include one blank page for each day of the vacation. Write the date at the top of each page. Note special events such as birthdays or anniversaries.

LEARNING BONUS: This summer journal provides an incentive for students to practice writing and to develop the knack of capturing important moments.

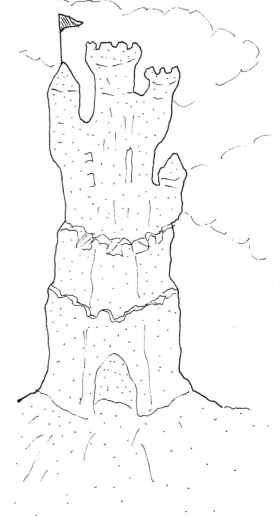

KEEP-ON-LEARNING LETTERS

Students write letters home, telling parents about important summertime learning activities.

STEPS TO SUCCESS:

1. Help students write a list of summer activities that will reinforce the skills—reading, writing, spelling, and so on—worked on during the school year. Examples of at-home projects are:

- letter writing
- reading for pleasure
- visiting museums
- starting a collection
- drawing or sketching
- conducting science experiments
- keeping a diary
- putting on puppet shows
- making a family tree
- doing fitness exercises
- solving crossword puzzles

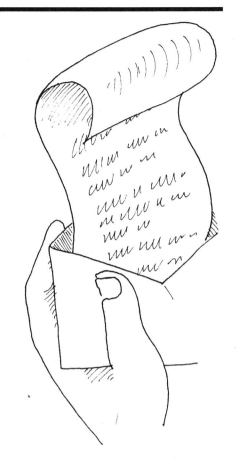

2. Have students write to their parents about four or five activities they might like to try. The letters should explain the importance of learning through the summer, and why the chosen activities are especially important.

3. Send the letters home before the last day of school, so that parent questions can be answered before vacation.

LEARNING BONUS: A summer learning letter usually comes from the teacher, but the communication is more meaningful when it involves student choice.

Dear Dad,

Things I want to do this summer:

- science experiments
- collect stamps
- visit museums
- make a family tree
- put on a puppet show
- keep a journal

MEMORY BOXES

Students create individual memory boxes to be opened a year or more in the future.

STEPS TO SUCCESS:

1. Ask each student to bring in a shoe box or similar container. Even a large mailing envelope might do.

2. Give students a series of short, daily writing assignments on topics such as:
- a word picture of me
- a person I admire
- how I think I might change in the future
- a new skill I would like to develop
- things I enjoy doing at home
- a place I would like to visit some day
- something I will never do again
- a letter to myself when I'm older

3. Encourage students to collect photographs, newspaper articles of interest, and other artifacts. For example, a sports fan might bring in a baseball card. A bookworm might choose a bookmark.

4. Have students put the writing and artifacts in their boxes, which should be sealed with tape or string. They should indicate when they will open their boxes.

5. Have students label their boxes with their names, the date for opening, other messages, and art.

6. Encourage students to find places at home where the boxes can be stored.

LEARNING BONUS: Creating memory boxes encourages students to look at themselves and think about their growth. Later, they'll have a chance to evaluate their predictions.

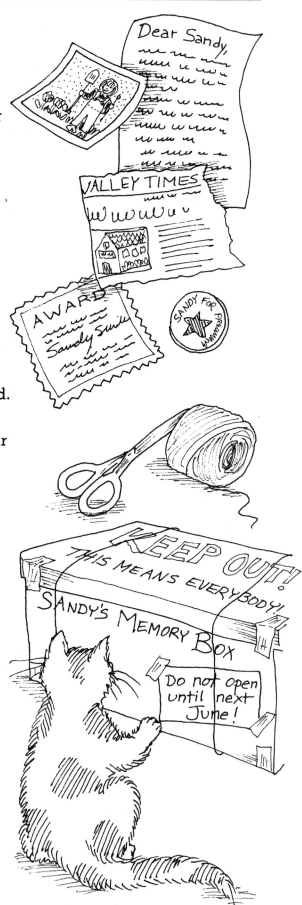

ANTI-BOREDOM BOOK

Students work together to prevent attacks by the Boredom Monster.

STEPS TO SUCCESS:

1. Brainstorm a list of activities that are fun to do when there's "nothing to do."

2. Have each student write about and illustrate one of the activities.

3. Appoint a committee to create a cover and title page for the book.

4. Photocopy the pages and make a book for each student.

5. Make the book available to other classes.

LEARNING BONUS: Cooperative problem solving produces many answers to the age-old vacation-time question, "What can I do now?"

Better get out the anti-boredom book for Tom!

ANTI-BOREDOM ACTIVITIES
Go away, I'm busy!
BOREDOM
WHEN THERE'S "NOTHING TO DO"

CRYSTAL BALL LETTERS

Students write letters to the next grade's students to learn what the grade will be like.

STEPS TO SUCCESS:

1. Find a class one grade above yours with students who will respond to a group letter from your students.

2. Help your students brainstorm a list of questions that they would like answered by students who are just finishing next year's grade. Examples might be:
- What books should we read over the summer?
- What were your favorite classroom activities?
- What field trips did you take?
- What's the hardest thing about _____ grade?

3. Compose a class letter to the older students. Include all the questions and ask for a prompt reply.

4. Assign a committee to deliver the letter. (If possible, work with more than one class. Comparing their responses could prove interesting.)

5. After the older students' responses have been read, encourage your students to write individual follow-up questions, as well as a class thank-you letter.

LEARNING BONUS: Students use their questioning skills to deal with the unknown. The older students have the positive experience of being experts.

CHAPTER 9

Saying Goodbye

FAREWELL LUNCHEON

Students produce a last-day-of-school class luncheon.

STEPS TO SUCCESS:

1. Help the class choose a time, setting, and theme for the luncheon. Possible themes are:
- alphabet foods (apples, bananas, carrots . . .)
- international foods
- foods our parents liked

2. Direct a small group of students to maintain a luncheon planning bulletin board. As each of the following steps is completed, the planning group will write up and post the results. This "working" board will help the class (and you) stay organized.

3. Create a menu appropriate for the theme. Have students look for the recipes.

4. Plan the food preparation. List both the needed equipment and ingredients.

5. Assign students the tasks of gathering the materials and/or preparing the food. Hint: Ask that all items be brought to school a day before the event—to head off the "Oh, I forgot . . . " problem.

6. Assign non-cooking jobs such as: decorating the room, writing the menu text (which might include interesting facts about the food), illustrating menus, creating place-names, and sending invitations to parent helpers.

7. Prepare a time line of tasks for the day of the luncheon. Include activities for students to do when not directly involved in luncheon preparation.

8. On luncheon day, have students follow the time line. When the meal is over, have students complete the Luncheon Evaluation Form (next page).

LEARNING BONUS: Students have the opportunity to use their organizational skills and to work together as a team for the last time.

LUNCHEON EVALUATION FORM

Evaluator's name:

1. My responsibilities were

2. The best part of the luncheon was

3. I wish we had

4. I wish we had not

5. The people I worked with were

6. I will always remember

Write other comments on the back of this sheet.

AUTOGRAPH BOOKS

Students create goodbye books.

STEPS TO SUCCESS:
1. If possible, share examples of old autograph rhymes and comments. Use your own, or try finding an anthology in the library.

2. Give directions for making a blank-page autograph book. Make available the following materials:
• cardboard plus wallpaper, felt, or construction paper for the cover
• colored paper for the pages
• yarn, staples, or rings for the binding

3. Brainstorm a list of possible titles, such as "Magical Memories" or "Friends Forever." Tell students to either compose their own titles or choose a title from the list.

4. Decide how and when students will collect autographs from classmates and the teacher.

5. Give students suggestions for what information to give and get, for example:
• signatures, addresses, and phone numbers
• sentence completions, such as, "I will always remember when . . . "
• autograph rhymes that say something particular about the person giving or getting the rhyme

LEARNING BONUS: This is a perfect activity for the last day of school. Students (and the teacher, too) leave for summer with a special memory book.

AUTOGRAPH! AUTOGRAPH! AUTOGRAPH! AUTOGRAPH! AUTOGRAPH! AUTOGRAPH!

OUR WILLS

Students reflect on their achievements by writing mini-essays in the form of a will.

STEPS TO SUCCESS:

1. Divide the class into small groups. Hand out the Will Planner (next page). Encourage the students to help each other think up at least five skills or kinds of knowledge to "leave" for incoming students.

2. Model the introductory paragraph for the students:

It is June 14, 19_____. I, _____, being of sound mind and body and ready to leave sixth grade, come to this place to write my will so that next year's class can know what they will need to be as successful as I was. However, if in the seventh grade I need any of what I willed here, I retain the right to take it back.

3. Tell the class to use the planning sheet to draft the body of their wills. Each will should have a minimum of five items, and each item should be described in two or three sentences:

I leave my knowledge of multiplication. You'll need it even if you own a good calculator.

4. After editing the introduction and body, have students make a final copy of their wills. For official-looking wills provide parchment paper and stick-on seals.

5. Save these wills to display on a September bulletin board for incoming students. Or have your students record them on tape.

LEARNING BONUS: By reviewing what has made them successful throughout the year, students become aware of their progress and their choices.

103

WILL PLANNER

Your name: _____

1. List five things you learned this year.

2. List five things you know how to do.

3. List five things you know about the teacher.

4. List three helpful behaviors you have, for example, remembering to put supplies away.

5. List four things you like to do in school.

6. List five happy memories you have from this year.

THANK-YOU NOTES

Students acknowledge the school staff for their contributions to the successful school year.

STEPS TO SUCCESS:

1. Lead the class in brainstorming a list of people who have helped the class during the school year. Here's a sample list from a fourth grade:

the principal
the special area teachers (music, art, etc.)
the school secretary
the custodian
the lunchroom supervisors
the bus drivers
the superintendent
the room parents
the teacher aides
the volunteers
the librarians
the textbook writers
the recess supervisor
the substitutes

2. Review the keys to writing a good thank-you note. The thank you should describe the gift or action and should explain why it was appreciated.

3. Let students choose the person to thank. Encourage them to work in pairs if there are more students than names on the list.

4. When their drafts have been edited, have the students copy their thank-you notes onto homemade stationery. The notes should be signed by the authors as representatives of the class.

5. Have students deliver the notes at least a week before the end of school in case the recipients wish to say thanks for the thanks.

LEARNING BONUS: Students are reminded that many people contribute to the success of a school. They also practice the thoughtful habit of acknowledging caring people.

LIBRARY GIFT PACK

Each student creates a learning gift for the school library.

STEPS TO SUCCESS:

1. Arrange for the students to visit the librarian and present the idea of giving a literary gift pack as their going away gift to the school.

2. Have the students and the librarian think up possible gifts. Try to balance the nitty-gritty needs of the library with the students' need to practice composition. Some ideas are:

- book jackets for jacketless fiction and nonfiction books
- instructional posters for using the card catalog, finding references, checking out books, and so on
- posters encouraging students to read all sorts of books, including poetry, drama, travel, fiction, and nonfiction
- a bulletin board with summaries of mystery books (without the ending, of course)
- local reference materials, such as maps of the area or old photos

3. Have each student choose a project.

4. Give students clear guidelines for writing and creating the gifts.

5. When all the projects are in final form, plan a gift-giving celebration in the library.

LEARNING BONUS: This activity gives students an opportunity to use their writing skills in a meaningful, generous way.

CALENDAR OF REPORT TOPICS

Many writing teachers believe that research should be a key part of the writing program. If you agree, you may be interested in the following list of three hundred report topics. The subjects are wide-ranging: famous people, inventions, explorations, places, events, catastrophes, and triumphs.

But there is a bonus. You'll notice that each topic is dated. This will enable you to use the calendar in carrying out a year-long research activity.

DAILY RESEARCH

The idea is simple. Every day, one child—or a small team—presents a short oral or written report on a topic related to that date in history.

Encourage your young reporters to gather their information from people as well as from books. For example, a report about the Wright Brothers might include facts from an interview with a pilot or even the pilot of a model plane. Each report might end with a list of the sources used.

If the reports are oral, consider limiting them to two or three minutes. Go for quality rather than quantity. Encourage the audience to take notes and to ask questions. If a question stumps the reporter, encourage him or her to do additional research and then make a follow-up presentation.

Don't stop there. By turning student-collected facts into a regular "Events in History" quiz, you'll show the class that you take their research efforts seriously.

You might also celebrate the research by preparing a monthly historical bulletin board. Each reporter or team can write a paragraph about an event, and then add an illustration. If the bulletin board is in the library, the students' efforts can contribute to the cultural literacy of the entire school.

A NOTE ABOUT ORIGINALITY

Copying from a reference book does little to sharpen research or writing skills. For a report to have value, students must go beyond the information which they collect. In order to do this, however, they probably will need some guidance. Here are some things you might suggest:

- Include something personal. In a report about the first use of ether (September 30), the student might talk about an operation he or she had in which an anaesthetic was used.

- Include an example. For instance, in a report about Steven Kellogg (October 6), the student might read a favorite passage from a Kellogg book, and then explain why the words are valued. A report about John Lennon might include an excerpt from a Lennon recording.

- Illustrate it. For example, a report about the sinking of the Titanic (April 14) might include the reporter's concept of the collision between the ship and the iceberg.

- Translate the information. Instead of presenting a prose version of an encyclopedia article, the student could get across the same ideas by writing a radio-drama script or a fictional diary or a rhyme.

- Extend it. For example, in a report about Jerrie Mock, the first woman to fly solo around the world (April 17), the student could list other famous women adventurers. A report about radar (June 24) could include a discussion of how police use radar to catch speeders, or it could mention the new stealth (anti-radar) technology. This kind of extension involves brainstorming, a key thinking skill.

SEPTEMBER

1 Jacques Cartier died, 1557
2 U.S. Treasury Department established, 1789
3 First professional football game, 1895
4 George Eastman patented camera, 1888
5 First *Clifford the Red Dog* book published, 1963
6 Harlem Globetrotters organized, 1927
7 Elizabeth I born, 1533
8 New Amsterdam renamed New York, 1664
9 "United Colonies" renamed United States, 1776
10 Elias Howe patented sewing machine, 1864
11 William Sydney Porter (O'Henry) born, 1862
12 Jesse Owens born, 1913
13 Walter Reed born, 1851
14 Francis Scott Key wrote "Star Spangled Banner," 1814
15 Tomie de Paolo born, 1934
16 Pilgrims set sail from England, 1620
17 U.S. Constitution adopted, 1787
18 The *New York Times* first published, 1851
19 Mickey Mouse appeared in his first cartoon, 1928
20 Alexander the Great born, 356 B.C.
21 H.G. Wells born, 1866
22 Raoul Wallenberg Day
23 Neptune discovered by Johann Galle, 1846
24 First atomic-powered aircraft carrier launched, 1960
25 Native Americans show Balboa the Pacific Ocean, 1513
26 John Chapman (Johnny Appleseed) born, 1774
27 Thomas Nast born, 1840
28 William the Conqueror invaded England, 1066
29 Enrico Fermi born, 1901
30 First use of ether, 1842

OCTOBER

1 First Model T sold, 1908
2 Mohandas Gandhi born, 1869
3 Universal Children's Day
4 Sputnik I put into orbit, 1957
5 Robert Goddard born, 1882
6 Steven Kellogg born, 1941
7 Rose chosen as U.S. national flower, 1986
8 Chicago fire, 1871
9 John Lennon born, 1940
10 Tuxedo introduced, 1886
11 Eleanor Roosevelt born, 1884
12 Columbus Day
13 Margaret Thatcher born, 1925
14 *Winnie the Pooh* published, 1926
15 Virgil born, 70 A.D. (World Poetry Day)
16 Noah Webster born, 1758
17 Henry Bessemer patented steel-making process, 1855
18 Alaska purchased from Russia, 1867
19 Benjamin Franklin proved lightning was electricity, 1752
20 Christopher Wren born, 1632
21 Alfred Nobel born, 1833
22 Sarah Bernhardt born, 1844
23 Gertrude Ederle became first woman to swim English Channel, 1906
24 United Nations' Day, 1945
25 Pablo Picasso born, 1881
26 Erie Canal opened, 1825
27 Theodore Roosevelt born, 1858
28 Statue of Liberty unveiled, 1886
29 New York Stock market collapsed, 1929
30 "War of the Worlds" broadcast, 1938
31 Halloween

NOVEMBER

1 Stephen Crane born, 1871
2 Daniel Boone born, 1734
3 First auto show opened, 1900
4 Howard Carter discovered King Tut's Tomb, 1922
5 Shirley Chisholm became first black woman elected to U.S. House of Representatives, 1968
6 Adolphe Sax born, 1814
7 Marie Curie born, 1884
8 First U.S. public library opened, 1781
9 Stagecoach service begun between New York and Philadelphia, 1756
10 Henry Stanley found David Livingston in Africa, 1871
11 Veteran's Day
12 Sun Yat-sen born, 1866
13 Robert Louis Stevenson born, 1850
14 Nellie Bly started on round-the-world trip, 1889
15 Georgia O'Keefe born, 1887
16 Oklahoma became 46th U.S. state, 1907
17 Suez Canal opened, 1869
18 Four time zones established for the U.S., 1881
19 Abe Lincoln gave the Gettysburg Address, 1863
20 Robert Kennedy born, 1925
21 Mayflower Compact signed, 1620
22 S.O.S. adopted as the international distress signal, 1908
23 Boris Karloff born, 1887
24 Barbed wire patented by Joseph Glidden, 1874
25 Carrie Nation born, 1864
26 Sojourner Truth Day
27 Charles Beard born, 1874
28 First auto race in U.S., 1895
29 Louisa May Alcott born, 1832
30 Mark Twain born, 1835

DECEMBER

1 First nuclear reaction demonstrated, 1942
2 Napoleon crowned himself emperor, 1804
3 First successful heart transplant, 1967
4 Vasili Kandinsky born, 1855
5 Walt Disney born, 1901
6 Thomas Edison made first sound recording, 1877
7 Pearl Harbor attacked, 1941
8 Eli Whitney born, 1765
9 First Christmas seals offered for sale, 1907
10 Emily Dickinson born, 1830
11 Indiana became the 19th U.S. state, 1816
12 First radio signal sent across the Atlantic, 1901
13 Sir Francis Drake started his voyage around the world, 1577
14 South Pole discovered, 1911
15 U.S. Bill of Rights ratified, 1791
16 Ludwig von Beethoven born, 1770
17 First successful airplane flight, 1903
18 Slavery ended in U.S. with ratification of 13th amendment, 1865
19 George Washington took army to Valley Forge, PA, 1777
20 Sacagawea died, 1812
21 Pilgrims landed at Plymouth Rock, 1620
22 Puccini born, 1858
23 Federal Reserve System established, 1913
24 Kit Carson born, 1809
25 Christmas Day
26 Boxing Day in England
27 Louis Pasteur born, 1822
28 Woodrow Wilson born, 1856
29 Wounded Knee Massacre, 1890
30 Rudyard Kipling born, 1865
31 New Year's Eve

JANUARY

1 Lincoln issued Emancipation Proclamation, 1863
2 Construction begun on Brooklyn Bridge, 1870
3 Lucretia Mott born, 1893
4 Louis Braille born, 1809
5 George Washington Carver born, 1864
6 Joan of Arc born, 1412
7 Galileo first saw Jupiter's moon, 1610
8 Elvis Presley born, 1935
9 First school for seeing eye dogs founded, 1929
10 League of Nations founded, 1920
11 Amelia Earhart began first solo flight across Pacific, 1935
12 Charles Perrault (editor of *Mother Goose*) born, 1628
13 National Geographic Society founded, 1888
14 Albert Schweitzer born, 1875
15 Martin Luther King born, 1929
16 NASA accepted first woman astronaut candidate, 1978
17 Benjamin Franklin born, 1706
18 Peter Roget (author of *Roget's Thesaurus*) born, 1779
19 Robert E. Lee born, 1807
20 First basketball game played in Springfield, MA, 1892
21 First atomic submarine Nautilus launched, 1954
22 Lord Byron born, 1788
23 Elizabeth Blackwell became first U.S. woman physician, 1849
24 John Sutter found gold near Sacramento, CA, 1848
25 Transcontinental telephone service inaugurated in U.S., 1915
26 First European settlers landed in Australia, 1788
27 Wolfgang Amadeus Mozart born, 1756
28 Space Shuttle Challenger exploded, 1986
29 W. C. Fields born, 1880
30 Franklin Delano Roosevelt born, 1882
31 Anna Pavlova born, 1885

FEBRUARY

1 Langston Hughes born, 1902
2 Groundhog Day
3 Norman Rockwell born, 1894
4 Charles Lindbergh born, 1902
5 National Wildlife Federation founded, 1936
6 Benjamin Banneker built the first chiming clock, 1754
7 Laura Ingalls Wilder born, 1867
8 Boy Scouts incorporated, 1910
9 U.S. Weather Service established, 1870
10 Leontyne Price born, 1927
11 Discovery of insulin announced in Toronto, 1922
12 Abraham Lincoln born, 1809
13 Chuck Yeager born, 1923
14 Frederick Douglass born, 1817
15 Susan B. Anthony born, 1820
16 First newspaper comic strip (Hogan's Alley) appeared, 1896
17 Marian Anderson born, 1902
18 Planet Pluto discovered, 1930
19 Nicolaus Copernicus born, 1473
20 John Glenn orbited the earth, 1962
21 Edwin Land introduced the Polaroid (60 second) Land Camera, 1947
22 George Washington born, 1732
23 George Frederick Handel born, 1685
24 Wilhelm Grimm born, 1786
25 Hiram Revels became first black U.S. Senator, 1870
26 Grand Canyon National Park established, 1919
27 Ralph Nader born, 1934
28 Linus Pauling born, 1901
29 Leap Year Day

MARCH

1 Car seat belts became mandatory, 1968
2 Theodore Geisel (Dr. Seuss) born, 1904
3 Alexander Graham Bell born, 1847
4 First meeting of U.S. Congress, 1789
5 Boston Massacre occurred, 1770
6 Michelangelo born, 1475
7 Janet Guthrie (first woman to race in Indy 500) born, 1938
8 Oliver Wendell Holmes born, 1841
9 Monitor and Merrimack Battle, 1862
10 Harriet Tubman Day
11 Mary Shelley published *Frankenstein*, 1818
12 First Girl Scout troup organized by Juliette Low, 1912
13 Planet Uranus discovered, 1781
14 Albert Einstein born, 1879
15 Julius Caesar assassinated, 44 B.C.
16 James Madison born, 1751
17 St. Patrick's Day
18 Rudolph Diesel born, 1858
19 First lunar eclipse recorded, 721 B.C.
20 *Uncle Tom's Cabin* published, 1852
21 Johann Sebastian Bach born, 1685
22 Marcel Marceau born, 1923
23 Patrick Henry delivered "Give me liberty or death" speech, 1775
24 Harry Houdini born, 1874
25 Gutson Borglum (Mt. Rushmore sculptor) born, 1871
26 Robert Frost born, 1874
27 Wilhelm Roentgen born, 1845
28 Three Mile Island nuclear plant malfunctioned, 1979
29 Last U.S. troops withdrew from Vietnam, 1973
30 Vincent Van Gogh born, 1853
31 Eiffel Tower completed, 1889

APRIL

1 April Fool's Day
2 Hans Christian Anderson born, 1805, International Book Day
3 Jane Goodall born, 1934
4 Dorthea Dix born, 1802
5 Booker T. Washington born, 1856
6 First modern Olympic Games held in Athens, Greece, 1896
7 William Wordsworth born, 1770
8 Ponce de Leon landed in Florida, 1513
9 First free public library in U.S., 1833
10 ASPCA founded, 1866
11 Jackie Robinson became first black major league baseball player, 1947
12 Beverly Cleary born, 1916
13 Thomas Jefferson born, 1743
14 Titanic hit iceberg and sank, 1912
15 Leonardo da Vinci born, 1452
16 Charlie Chaplin born, 1889
17 First woman (Jerrie Mock) flew solo around world, 1964
18 Paul Revere's ride, 1775
19 Revolutionary War began, 1775
20 Romulus founded Rome, 753 B.C.
21 Queen Elizabeth II born, 1926
22 Arbor Day
23 William Shakespeare born, 1564
24 Library of Congress created, 1800
25 Ella Fitzgerald born, 1918
26 John James Audubon born, 1785
27 Samuel F.B. Morse born, 1791
28 Mutiny on H.M.S. Bounty, 1789
29 First electric streetlights, Cleveland, Ohio, 1879
30 First commercial TV broadcast, 1939

MAY

1 Empire State Building opened to the public, 1931
2 Jetliner passenger service begun, 1952
3 Golda Meir born, 1895
4 Horace Mann born, 1796
5 Cinco de Mayo in Mexico
6 Civil Rights Act passed, 1960
7 Peter Tchaikovsky born, 1840
8 V-E Day, 1945
9 James Barrie born, 1860
10 Transcontinental railroad completed, 1869
11 Irving Berlin born, 1888
12 Florence Nightingale born, 1820
13 Joe Louis born, 1914
14 Israel became nation, 1948
15 L. Frank Baum (author of *Wizard of Oz*) born, 1900
16 First Oscars awarded, 1929
17 New York Stock Exchange opened, 1792
18 Massachusetts passed first compulsory school attendance law, 1852
19 Ringling Brothers circus opened, 1884
20 Levi Strauss patented denim pants, 1873
21 First nuclear-powered lighthouse began operating, 1964
22 First modern atlas published, 1570
23 Mary Cassatt born, 1844
24 Peter Minuit bought Manhattan Island, 1626
25 Ralph Waldo Emerson born, 1802
26 Sally Ride born, 1950
27 Golden Gate Bridge opened, 1937
28 Dionne Quintuplets born, 1934
29 Edmund Hillary and Tenzing Norkay were first climbers to reach summit of Mt. Everest, 1953
30 Tomb of unknown soldier dedicated, 1921
31 Walt Whitman born, 1819

JUNE

1 Brigham Young born, 1801
2 Martha Washington born, 1732
3 "Casey at the Bat" published, 1888
4 Henry Ford drove first Ford car, 1896
5 Richard Scarry born, 1919
6 D-Day, 1944
7 Gwendolyn Brooks born, 1917
8 Frank Lloyd Wright born, 1869
9 Cole Porter born, 1893
10 Maurice Sendak born, 1928
11 King Kamehameha Day
12 Baseball Hall of Fame opened in Cooperstown, NY, 1939
13 Alexander the Great died, 323 B.C.
14 Flag Day
15 Magna Carta granted, 1215
16 First woman in space, 1963
17 Iceland became an independent republic, 1944
18 Napoleon defeated at Waterloo, 1815
19 Garfield comic strip first appeared, 1978
20 Great Seal of U.S. adopted, 1782
21 First long-playing record produced, 1948
22 Voting age in U.S. lowered from 21 to 18, 1970
23 Wilma Rudolph born, 1940
24 Radar first used to detect planes, 1930
25 Custer's Last Stand, 1876
26 Pearl Buck born, 1892
27 Helen Keller born, 1880
28 Peace Treaty of Versailles signed, 1919
29 Peter Paul Rubens born, 1577
30 Zaire established, 1960

This Calendar of Report Topics is just a beginning. Encourage your students to suggest other dates to enrich your calendar for future years.